This book belongs to

Thank you to all the hard working, creative, and inspirational minds that were involved in the creation of this revolutionary and experiential book. This book is dedicated to all the readers who have the imagination and passion for learning and adventure.

Truly,

Scott Jochim

President

POPAR™

Read it. See it. Be it.

Digital Tech Frontier, LLC. Arizona

www.PoparToys.com

Digital Tech Frontier, LLC.
2730 S. Hardy DR. Ste. #1, Tempe, AZ 85282

ISBN 978-0-6530127-1-9

Text and Design by Robert Siddell
Production and Design by Scott Jochim
3D art and Animations by Shrox
3D art and Animations by Montrose Edmonds
3D art, Animations, Graphic Design by Rick Muniz
Graphic Design by Chrissie Vales

Printed in China

Table of Contents

Tools Needed To Explore These Bugs

1 Go to www.PoparToys.com/software

2 Find the software that matches this book

3 Download and install the software

Remove the "i" paddle to use throughout the entire book

What are the minimum computer system requirements to view Augmented Reality in Popar™ Books?

PC Hardware:
•A webcam
•CPU-Pentium 3 800MHz or higher processor. 1200MHz recommended
•RAM-500 MB or above recommended
•Graphics card-3D accelerated graphics card
PC Operating System:
•Windows XP SP2 or above, Windows Vista, Windows 7

Droid:
•Droid 4.0 or Higher

Macintosh Hardware:
•A webcam
•CPU-Intel Core 2 Duo 2.0 GHz or above
•RAM-500 MB or above recommended
•Graphics card-3D accelerated graphics card
Mactintosh Operating System:
•Mac OS 10.4, 10.5 and 10.6

IOS:
•iPhone 4/4s, iPad 2/3 or Higher

HERE'S HOW IT WORKS !!!...

What are Popar™ Books?
Popar™ Books use Augmented Reality (AR) technology to create an immersive reading experience that will allow the user to see their books come alive with incredible virtually "real" 3D objects and animations that will pop off the page. Popar™ Books are designed to change the way we interact and experience stories, adventures, and learning.

What is Augmented Reality (AR)?
Our Augmented Reality (AR) is a ground-breaking concept that uses a webcam and computer, or a mobile device, and special black and white patterned markers to make amazing 3D objects and animations appear in the real world that provide a high degree of engaging interaction that maintain interest in all of the Popar™ Book series.

What do I need to see Augmented Reality in my Popar™ Book?
- Computer or mobile device that meets the minimum system requirements
- A webcam or mobile device
- Popar™ Books software
- Popar™ Books

1

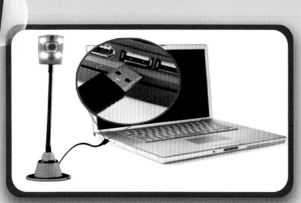

First, you will need to hook up your webcam to your computers USB.
*Note: For mobile users see step 2.

2

Then download the Popar™ Books installation software from www.PoparToys.com/software.
*Note: Mobile users download the Popar™ Bugs 3D Book app.

3

Run the Popar™ Books software

4

Go to page three and take out the "i" paddle. *Note: "i" paddle is not needed with mobile devices.

5

Next position your webcam or mobile device, so that it has a view of the entire Popar™ Book when the book is open.

READ-ALONG INSTRUCTIONS

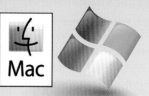

Mac

*Note: Mobile users see in app tutorial for read along instructions

A

On the bottom of every single right hand page is a black & white Augmented Reality (AR) marker that will display a 3D animation when in view of the webcam.

B

In order to start the read-along feature on every page, the black & white Augmented Reality marker and the "i" paddle must both be in view of the webcam. Simply bring the "i" paddle close to the Augmented Reality marker or close to the center of the page in order for the book to be read to you.

C

Do not overlap the black and white Augmented Reality markers or the animation and model will not appear.

D

Before

After

Grasshopper

Food:

The grasshopper is an amazing insect that can leap 20 times the length of its own body. If we could do that, we would be able to jump almost 40 yards! They live in fields, meadows, and just about anywhere they can find generous amounts of leaves to eat. Some types of grasshoppers will only eat certain types of plants. Grasshoppers can destroy entire crops of alfalfa, clover, cotton, corn, and other grains, causing millions of dollars in crop damages every year.

Cool Fact:

Short horned grasshoppers have ears in the sides of the abdomen. Long-horned grasshoppers and crickets have ears in the knee-joints of their front legs.

Most grasshoppers lead relatively blameless lives, causing little harm to crops or gardens. However, some species of grasshoppers can change into a very damaging form indeed, in which they congregate in huge swarms that can do severe damage to crops. These swarming grasshoppers are called locusts.

Swarms

Hop

Hop

Hop

Hop

Singing

A very attractive feature of some grasshoppers is their ability to sing. Males do the singing, and they do it to attract female mates, or to warn off other males. There are two different mechanisms for singing. In one (used by short-horned grasshoppers), there is a comb-like structure with a row of teeth on the inside of the hind leg, which gets rubbed against a ridge on the wing. This produces a "chirp" sound. Crickets and long-horned grasshoppers also have a comb-and-ridge mechanism, located on the left and right forewings, that creates a chirp sound when rubbed together.

FUN FACT

Grasshopper

When a grasshopper is picked up, they "spit" a brown liquid which is known by most kids and adults as "tobacco juice." Some scientists believe that this liquid may protect grasshoppers from attacks by insects such as ants.

Centipede

A centipede is a common name for the members of the class Chilopoda that also includes crustaceans, insects, and spiders. Centipedes are long, segmented animals with jointed appendages and a poisonous "bite."

Appearance:

The body is 1 to 1 1/2 inch long, but its legs make the centipede appear to seem much larger. The body is grayish-yellow with three dark stripes extending along the full length of the back. The legs are long in proportion to the body size, and they have alternate light and dark bands running around them.

Unlike most other centipedes, the house centipede generally lives its entire life inside a building. This centipede will prefer to live in damp areas such as cellars, closets, bathrooms, attics (during the warm months), and unexcavated areas under the house.

Squirm

Squirm

Squirm

Squir

Food:

The house centipede forages at night for small insects and their larvae. From a control tool point of view, they can be beneficial in controlling other insects.

Life Cycle:

They develop by gradual metamorphosis, so immature centipedes have a similar appearance to adults but are smaller. Eggs are laid in the damp places that they live in, as well as behind baseboards or beneath bark on firewood.

Cool Fact:

Although the centipede can bite, its jaws are quite weak. There usually is not more than a slight swelling if a bite occurs.

FUN FACT

Centipede

Most centipedes are 2.5 to 5 cm (1 to 2 in) long, but some tropical species grow to 30 cm (12 in).

POPAR Read it. See it. Be it.

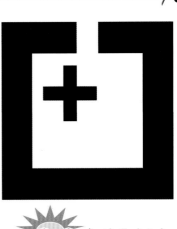

POPAR Read it. See it. Be it.

9

Butterfly

Butterfly wings are made of tiny scales that create beautiful colors and striking patterns. The dark colors help the butterfly keep warm by absorbing heat from sunlight. Because they are cold-blooded, butterflies cannot produce their own body heat. There are about 24,000 species of butterflies, and they can be found in every part of the world except in Antarctica.

During their lifetimes, butterflies change form three times - from egg to caterpillar to chrysalis to butterfly. This is called metamorphosis. When the caterpillar hatches from the egg, all it wants to do is eat. So much weight is gained, that the butterfly has to shed its skin four or five times. The last shed produces a hard case called a chrysalis or pupa. Some species wrap themselves in silk before they change to a chrysalis for extra protection. Though not visible, a dramatic change takes place inside the chrysalis; the caterpillar changes into a butterfly.

Poisonous butterflies, by their bright colors, warn predators like bats, mice, wasps, birds, and lizards to stay away. Other butterflies use camouflage to hide in plain sight. And still others that are nonpoisonous try to copy the look of poisonous types to fool predators into leaving them alone. "Because they cannot survive a winter in the cold climate, in autumn, millions of Monarchs fly thousands of miles south to roost in trees in mountainous areas of California and Mexico."

Cool Facts:

Butterflies range in size from 1/25 inch to 10 inches. Butterflies can see red, green, and yellow.

Flutter

FUN FACT

Butterfly

There is around 24,000 or more species of butterflies around the world. Probably the biggest is the Queen Alexandra's Birdwing that lives in the rain forests of Papua, New Guinea. It has a wingspan of 11 inches and is poisonous.

Bee

About 20,000 species of bees exist, varying from minute forms only 2 mm (0.08 in) long to large insects that are 4 cm (1.6 in) long. Bees are divided into a number of families, largely on the basis of mouth parts and other characteristics that are difficult to see without dissection. Although most do not have a distinctive appearance to set them apart, families are the basic subdivisions of the Apoidea.

Queen Bees

The queen is the only sexually developed female in the hive. The queen mates in flight with approximately 18 drones. She only mates once in her lifetime. A queen can lay 3,000 eggs in a day, and up to 200,000 eggs in a year. Queens can live for up to two years.

Cool Fact:

A single hive contains approximately 40-45,000 bees.

HONEY

Bees have been producing honey for at least 150 million years. The honeycomb is composed of hexagonal cells with walls that are only 2/1000 inch thick, but support 25 times their own weight. Honey is nectar that bees have repeatedly regurgitated and dehydrated. To make one pound of honey, workers in a hive fly 55,000 miles and tap two million flowers.

Buzz

Buzz

Buzz

Honeybees communicate with one another by dancing in order to give the direction and distance of flowers.

- Bees possess five eyes.
- Honeybees can perceive movements that are separated by 1/300th of a second. Humans can only sense movements separated by 1/50th of a second.
- Were a bee to enter a cinema, it would be able to differentiate each individual movie frame being projected.
- Bees cannot recognize the color red.
- Honeybees' stingers have a barb which anchors the stinger in the victim's body.
- The bee leaves its stinger and venom pouch behind, and soon dies from abdominal rupture.
- Africanized Honey Bees (killer bees) will pursue an enemy 1/4 mile or more.

FUN FACT

Bee

The energy in one ounce of honey would provide one bee with enough energy to fly around the world.

Ant

Some 9,500 species of ants have been discovered and named so far. Ants have been around for about 100 million years, and are found in just about every type of land environment.

Colonies:

Ants are social insects that live together in large groups or colonies. Their group home is usually a system of underground tunnels and chambers, with mounds above the surface that are formed out of the dirt or sand they removed in digging.

Each ant has a specific job. The queen lays eggs to populate the colony. Workers collect food, feed members of the colony, and enlarge the nest. Soldiers are large workers that defend the colony and sometimes attack ants who are strangers. All these hard-working ants are female. Males have wings to fly to another colony, where they mate with a queen and die soon afterwards.

Food:

Ants are very fond of eating sweet foods, seeds, and other insects. Sweets provide energy for worker ants, and the protein from other insects helps build up the ant's body. Harvester ants collect and store seeds. Leaf-cutter ants grow fungus for food.

Cool Facts:

An ant can lift 50 times its own weight—that is as much a feat for them as lifting a car would be for you!

Ants communicate by touching each other with their antennae. They show other ants where food is by making a path with a chemical (called a pheromone) that leaves a scent that the ants follow.

FUN FACT

Ant

The world's biggest ant colony was discovered in 2002. This super colony has billions of ants living in millions of nests. It stretches 3,600 miles, all the way from Italy to northwest Spain.

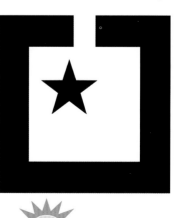

POPAR Read it. See it. Be it.

Tarantula

The name tarantula is given to a group of large spiders with hairy bodies and legs. There are approximately 900 species found in most of the world's tropical, subtropical, and arid regions. They vary in color and behavior according to their specific environments. Generally, however, tarantulas are burrowers that live in the ground.

The largest tarantula is the Goliath bird-eating tarantula, while the smallest is the size of a fingernail. These spiders have many different regional names, including "baboon spiders" in Africa and "bird-eating spiders" or "earth tigers" in Asia. Some species native to Australia are referred to as "whistling spiders" or "barking spiders."

Cool Fact:

Females will sit and guard a cocoon for six to nine weeks; 500 to 1,000 tarantulas may hatch.

Food:

Tarantulas are slow and deliberate movers, but accomplished nocturnal predators. Insects are their main prey, but they also target bigger game including frogs, toads, and mice.

Predator

Tarantulas have natural enemies, parasitic pepsis wa are an exception. S a wasp will paraly: tarantula with its s and lay its eggs on spider's body. When eggs hatch, wasp lar gorge themselves on still living tarantula

FUN FACT

Tarantula

Tarantula venom is weaker than that of a honeybee and, though painful, is virtually harmless to humans.

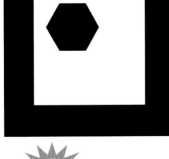

Scorpion

Scorpion is the common name for any member of the ARTHROPOD order Scorpionida, class Arachnida. This class also includes spiders and mites. About 1400 species of scorpion exist; about 40 of them occur in the U.S. Usually brown in color and ranging from about 2.5 to 20 cm (about 1 to 8 in) in length, the scorpion has a flat, narrow body, two lobster like claws, eight legs, and a segmented abdominal tail. A scorpion's tail contains a venomous stinger supplied by a pair of poison glands. The tail is usually curved upward and forward over the back.

Vision.

Despite having six to twelve eyes, scorpions do not have good eyesight. However, they can readily distinguish light from dark and appear to have excellent low light sensitivity, which helps them to both avoid harsh sunlight and to navigate by starlight or moonlight. They sense their way around using sensory hairs and slit organs on the legs that pick up vibrations and scents. They also have special organs on the underside of the body called pectines that pick up ground textures and scents.

Scorpions also turn fluorescent under ultraviolet light that is a good way for scientists to find them in the field. The fluorescence is caused by an unidentified substance in a very thin layer in the cuticle of the scorpion called the "hyaline layer." The fluorescence is thought to serve as an ultraviolet sensitivity mechanism, perhaps allowing the scorpion to avoid damaging light levels.

FUN FACT

Scorpion

The female scorpion carries the pale young scorpions on her back for the first few days or weeks, until they are strong enough to become independent.

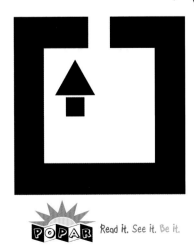

POPAR Read it. See it. Be it.

Dragonfly

Dragonflies have a very short lifespan. They usually only live for about a month or less. However, some dragonflies can exist for up to half a year.

If you see a dragonfly, more than likely you saw it near a pond, lake, stream, swamp, river, or even a rain puddle. They begin their lives in water, and because they have such a short lifespan, you will usually see them near water. Some dragonflies do wander off into forests and fields to search for food, but will return to the water to mate and lay eggs.

Food:

Dragonflies usually eat mosquitoes, bees, gnats, butterflies, termites, and other bugs. When they are in the nymph stage, they eat small fish, tadpoles, mosquito larvae, worms, and aquatic insects.

Vision:

Dragonflies have very big eyes for their body's proportion. They use their huge eyes to hunt bugs, and allows them to be able to spot prey at a distance. Because their eyes are curve-shaped, they can see in several different directions at a time.

The majority of dragonflies have an average wingspan of about three to four inches long. Some have a wingspan of about six inches long. There is a group of the smallest dragonflies that have a wingspan of only 7/10 of an inch.

Predators:

Dragonflies are often hunted by spiders, snakes, birds, frogs, and other animals. They are often eaten in mid-air by birds. They can also become the meals for spiders when they get trapped in a spider web.

FUN FACT

Dragonfly

The legs of dragonflies are great for capturing their prey. However, they are not strong enough for walking.

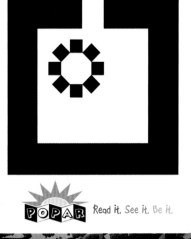

POPAR Read it. See it. Be it.

Fireflies

Fireflies are soft-bodied beetles whose sizes range from 5 to 25 millimeters in length. On the underside of the abdomen, fireflies have special light organs that glow in luminous flashes. The flattened, dark brown or black body is often marked with yellow or orange. Most of the fireflies feed on pollen and nectar'but adult fireflies do not eat at all.

Females:

The female fireflies will produce a short rhythmic flash that attracts the male fireflies. The females will sit on the ground in the high grass to flash to a certain male only. The female chooses the males based on their flash pattern.

Cool Fact:

How is the firefly light produced? This process is called bioluminescene. To do this, the fireflies contain specialized cells in their abdomen that make light.

There are a few different reasons why fireflies glow. One of the most generally accepted reasons is that a firefly will use their glow as a warning signal that communicates to potential predators that they taste bad because they have defensive chemicals in their bodies. Another reason is that in most species-specific of North American fireflies, during a certain time of night, males fly about flashing their species specific flash pattern. If a flashing male catches a female's eye, she will respond after the last male's flash indicates where she is located.

FUN FACT

Fireflies

Fireflies do not bite, do not have pinchers, do not carry disease and in fact are quite harmless. They cannot even fly fast. They have a life span of two months.

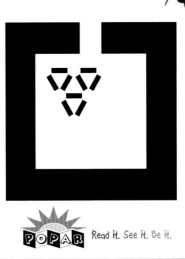

POPAR Read it. See it. Be it.

Praying Mantis

Mantodea or mantises is an order of insects that contains approximately 2,200 species in nine families worldwide in temperate and tropical habitats. Praying mantis is named for its prominent front legs that are bent and held together at an angle that suggests the position of prayer. The larger group of these insects is more properly called the "praying mantids." Mantis refers to the genus mantis, to which only some "Praying Mantids" belong.

Food:

Praying mantids are highly predacious and feed on a variety of insects including moths, crickets, grasshoppers, and flies. They lie in wait with the front legs in an upraised position. They intently watch and stalk their prey. They will eat each other as well.

Habitat:

Praying mantids are often protectively colored to the plants they live on. This camouflage allows them to be invisible to their prey. Mantids are usually found on plants that have other insects around. Some mantids live in grass. Winged adults may be attracted to black lights in late summer and early fall.

Baby Mantid's

A distinct, styrofoam-like egg case protects Mantid eggs throughout the winter. Up to 200 or more nymphs may emerge from the egg case. The nymphs look like adults except for size, sexual definition, and a possible difference in coloration and pattern.

FUN FACT

Praying Mantis

The mantid's strike takes an amazing 30 to 50 one-thousandths of a second. The strike is so fast that it cannot be processed by the human brain.

Ladybug

The ladybug, or Coccinellidae, has six jointed legs, a pair of antennae, and the three-part body, all consistent with the insect species. However, the ladybug happens to be one of the best loved insects in the world. Children love ladybugs as they are easy to catch and are brightly colored.

There are over 450 species of ladybugs in North America alone. While many of these are native, some were brought into the area from other countries. There are more than 5,000 different ladybug species in the world. While they are usually of a red or orange coloring with black markings, there are some that are black with reddish colored markings, and some may have yellow coloring. Most Ladybugs feed chiefly on aphids and other small insects, but there are also several forms that feed on plants. The ladybug is also called a ladybeetle, ladybird beetle, and ladybird.

Cool Fact:
Their red backs are really wing cases that protect the delicate wings folded up beneath them.

Name:
During the Middle Ages, swarms of pests were destroying crops, so farmers prayed to the Virgin Mary, the mother of Jesus, for help. Soon after, ladybugs came and ate the bad pests and saved the crops. The farmers called these bugs, "Beetles of Our Lady" and they eventually became known as "ladybugs."

The most common American ladybug has seven spots.

predator

There is research indicating that ladybugs probably do taste bad to predators, and that they may even produce a foul-smelling odor from a fluid from joints in their legs. When threatened, ladybugs "play dead." Many predators will not eat an insect that does not move, so this is another way that the ladybug protects itself from danger.

FUN FACT

Ladybug

The Ladybug is the state insect for Massachusetts, New Hampshire, Ohio, Tennessee, and Delaware.

Digital Toys Here

1

Cut out Popar™
Paddles on pages
29 and 30

2

Play with Popar™
Paddles

Need Help? Go to www.PoparToys.com for tech support.

28

Read it. See it. Be it.
Read it. See it. Be it.
Read it. See it. Be it.
Read it. See it. Be it.
Read it. See it. Be it.
Read it. See it. Be it.

Cut out or photocopy Popar™ Paddles on this page and the next page. Use these paddles with the web camera or mobile device and software when you are not reading the book. The Popar™ Paddles have the same amazing 3D objects, just like in the story. These 3D digital toys are great to play with, take photos or capture video to share with your friends and family.

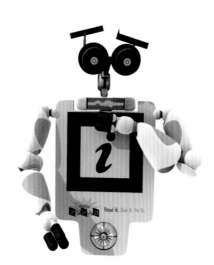

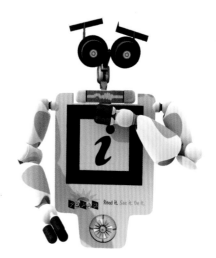

POPAR™ Read it. See it. Be it.

The Augmented Reality "i" paddle that MARC-E is pointing at is what you will use throughout the entire Popar™ Books series to trigger the interaction with the 3D objects in the book or on the paddles above. These animations can be initiated by simply holding the "i" paddle close to any of the black and white symbols.

Get ready to...

Read it. See it. Be it!